# girlfriends

## (from campfires to crow's feet)

other books
by monica sheehan

_____

the breakup book

50 reasons not
to go home
for the holidays

# girlfriends
## (from campfires to crow's feet)

# by monica sheehan

**Andrews McMeel
Publishing**

Kansas City

01 02 03 04 05 BIN 10 9 8 7 6 5 4 3 2 1

ISBN: 0-7407-1879-7
Library of Congress Catalog Card Number: 2001086442

Attention: Schools and Businesses
Andrews McMeel books are available at quantity discounts with bulk purchase
for educational, business, or sales promotional use. For information, please
write to: Special Sales Department, Andrews McMeel Publishing,
4520 Main Street, Kansas City, Missouri 64111.

## to all my girlfriends ...

mary jane, ann, nora, sarah,
bea, aunt ann, mary, megan, dina,
marianne, kelly, sheila, allie, barb
carrie, susan, tina, holly, bonnie,
pat, steph, lynne, maureen,
margaret, abby, megan s., sarah k.,
molly, abigail, caitlin, nora b.,
kara, and meredith.

# acknowledgments

i'd like to thank mary jane,
nora, margaret, and tina for all their
support; mary mullane, tim, and maureen
for their funny submissions;
megan sheehan, my favorite writer,
who generously gave her time, brilliant
ideas, and delicate suggestions;
and, last but not least, my editor,
jean lucas, for making this possible.


and a special thanks
to mike hubert, for putting up with
the insane deadlines and the tears,
and caring about my little cartoons.

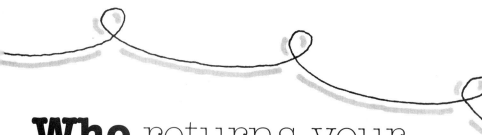

**Who** returns your calls faster than a speeding bullet?

**Who** leaps to your side in a single bound?

**Whose** friendship is more powerful than a locomotive?

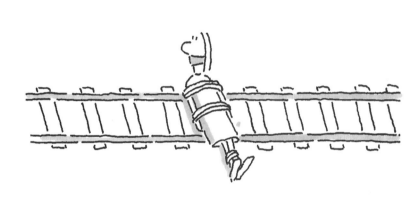

It's your **mother?**

It's your
**hairdresser?**

It's your **dog?!**

# No!!
# It's your girlfriend!

**Girlfriends** have been around since the beginning of time ...

and throughout
history.

There always has
and always
will be **girlfriends.**

The **world**
wouldn't be the
same without
them ...

and neither
would **we.**

the beginning

# childhood...

maybe she was the girl
next door. maybe she sat
next to you at the blue
table in kindergarten.
the connection was
immediate. she loved the
color purple. she hated
peas. and her parents
wouldn't let her get a
pony, either. what a thrill.
someone like you. your
first real girlfriend. no

more being prisoner in the back of your mother's station wagon or having to play the insignificant supporting role of the dog in your brother's torturous games. your own life was beginning. together you would strike your independence. there were games to play, cookies to make, and secrets to keep.

**Girlfriends** pick you first for kickball.

**Girlfriends**
hold hands
jumping off the
diving board.

**Girlfriends** don't mind if you give their Barbie a haircut (or lose one of her shoes).

**Girlfriends**
make plans to be
princesses, have
ponies, and get
married at the
exact same time.

# growing up ...

time to put away the bar-
bies and get out the blow
dryer. you've crossed the
threshold, ready or not.
thank the heavens above
you have your girlfriend
to lead the way. she tells
you of the joys of tampons
and commiserates about
curfews. your childhood
bedrooms, now studio
apartments, becoming
the fashion runways, the

dance studios, and after-hour clubs. talking about who made the team and who was making out. the two of you, charting unknown territory of bras, boys, and beer (and, of course, high school). if you stuck together and wore the right outfits you would make it (and afterward, maybe even cross-country). but now it was time to get the grades and get out.

**Girlfriends**
meet you for a
cigarette before
biology.

**Girlfriends** bring you to the best parties.

**Girlfriends**
help you
cram for your
history final.

true blue

# true blue . . .

the kind of girlfriends you couldn't live without. the ones whose loyalty and love are unquestionable. she's your sister, your mother, your shrink, and your personal trainer all wrapped up in one. the person who you can "just be" with. the love, laughter, and time are the glue that's kept you together and always will. she knows you

better than you know your-
self and isn't afraid to say
so. you've been through
hell and hairstyles together.
true blue girlfriends are
the ones who talk about
everything and nothing for
two and a half hours, who
buy when you're broke,
who pick you up and push
you in the right direction.
a bond that transcends
time and geography. one
that is, in fact, you.

**Girlfriends** provide a nonthreatening environment for self-discovery.

**Girlfriends** share their M&M's, magazines, and Xanax.

**Girlfriends**
are always
happy to spy.

**Girlfriends** know all about their fashion do's and don'ts.

**Girlfriends**
lie to your mother
for you.

**Girlfriends** endure two-hour play-by-play conversations about your hopeless relationships.

**Girlfriends** know when it's time to "see if it's in the cards."

**Girlfriends** know
how to
keep a secret.

**Girlfriends** always provide the silver lining.

**Girlfriends** know when to get away from it all.

**Girlfriends** know the only men you've been to bed with in last six months are Ben & Jerry.

**Girlfriends** know when you're feeling small.

**Girlfriends** skip "the roll" at lunch, so they can have "the wine" with dinner.

**Girlfriends** know when you're lying.

**Girlfriends** know the best things in life are "flea."

**Girlfriends** tell your husband your new leather jacket was half price.

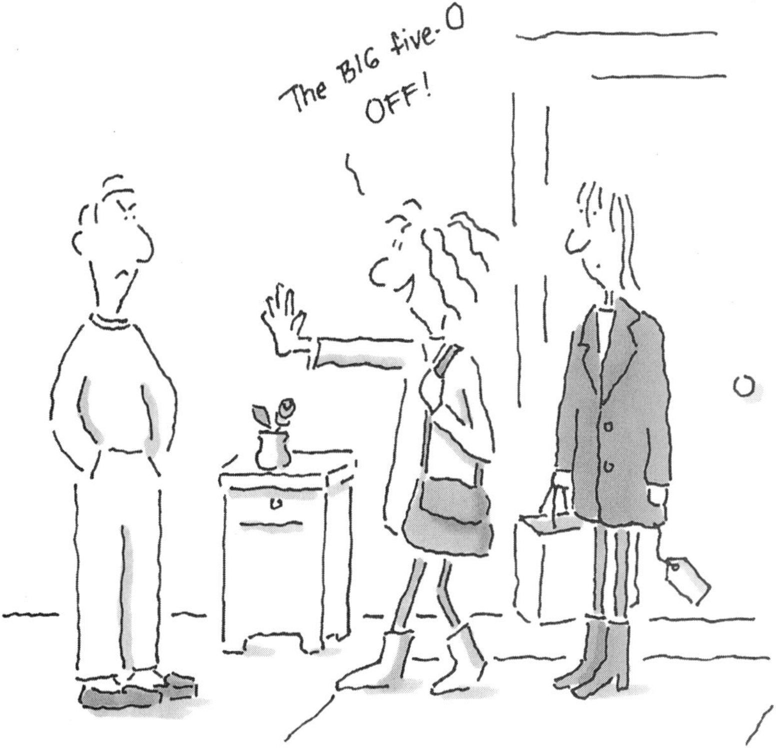

The BIG five-0
OFF!

# Girlfriends
sometimes
break up ...

but not for long.

# a word about the rituals...

the importance of rituals in our lives has been recognized by the great minds of our time, but girlfriends have known it all along. to start, the phone calls. daily. sometimes three to four times daily. lunch. splitting everything (the burger, the california roll, the french fries, the crème brûlée, the bill).

the manicures. girls' night out. pigging out. chilling out. working out. dishing it out. frivolous to some, cherished by others. it may not be high mass, but we are devoted to these little rites. after all, fire-red nail polish has inspired an epiphany or two. it's in the sharing of what's between you, like that plate of greasy french fries, that's the best.

**Girlfriends** seek nirvana through seaweed masks and sultry nail polish.

**Girlfriends** will take a u-turn off the road to health in a split second.

**Girlfriends** help find the "perfect" coat, couch, and carpeting.

**Girlfriends** pledge allegiance to the cosmetic counters of america.

**Girlfriends** pick up
the phone
in the middle
of the night.

**Girlfriends** get together for dinner and a movie.

**Girlfriends** stay at the beach till sundown.

**Girlfriends** are
a conversation . . .

that never ends.

Monica Sheehan is a freelance artist living on the Jersey Shore. She has illustrated twelve books, including cowriting *50 Reasons Not to Go Home for the Holidays*, and creating *The Breakup Book*. She presently has a monthly feature in *Real Simple* magazine. Ms. Sheehan's work has also appeared in the *Chicago Tribune*, the *New York Times*, and *Woman's Day*.